Color With Your Besties
Sherri Baldy
Coloring Books

About The Artist

Sherri Baldy is known for her trademark Big Eyed art for over 20 plus years around the world. She is a multi media artist that is licensed on a wide range of products. Sherri lives in Riverside, Calif. with her husband on their farm (Urban Farm Diva Farms) She has two sons Kyler & Josh & two daughters Courtney & Brittany.

When she is not painting, drawing and creating craft products for the craft industry, she spends her time in the gardens at the farm and in her "Barn Studio" that is open to the public by appointment. Sherri Baldy is now offering her Big Eyed My-Bestie artwork in coloring books.

Come visit with Sherri and her Besties on one of her crafting Facebook Group. www.facebook.com/groups/mybestiesdesigns or visit Sherri in her coloring book group at: www.facebook/groups/116425085645132 See Back page for Sherri's fun patreon clubs.

www.MyBestiesShop.com
Sherri Baldy My Besties Coloring Books in Riverside CA.
Copyright Sherri Baldy ~ My-Besties TM

I'm Not Sassy Just HOT Flashy!

I'm Not Sassy Just HOT Flashy!

WHEN YOUR HOT YOUR HOT!!!

WHEN YOUR HOT YOUR HOT!!!

Cool It!

Cool it!

© Sherri Baldy My-Besties

TOO HOT TO HANDLE!

TOO HOT TO HANDLE!

HOT Oh So Flashy!

HOT Oh So Flashy!

TOOO HOT
+
TOOO
FLASHY!

TOOO HOT
+
TOOO
FLASHY!

Hot
Flashes
&
Cocktails

Hot
Flashes
&
Cocktails

What A Girl Won't Do To Cool Down!

What A Girl Won't Do To Cool Down!

CAUTION MENOPAUSAL WOMAN!

CAUTION MENOPAUSAL WOMAN!

HOT!
Cold!
Make Up
Your Mind!

HOT!
Cold!
Make Up
Your Mind!

Color With Your Besties
Sherri Baldy
Coloring Books

Welcome to My Besties World!
Sherri invites you to come join in her SUPER
Friendly and FUN Crafting community!
We always look forward to seeing ALL the Sherri
Baldy My-Besties Creations by our coloring, crafter
friends from all around the world and We LOVE
meeting and making NEW Friends!
Come PARTY with us every few weeks at our FB
FUN NEW Releases where we have Loads of
Giveaways, Name Games going on and Freebies!!!
We share tips, tricks and techniques. Join in on the
FUN coloring & crafting group here:
https://www.facebook.com/groups/mybestiesdesign
s/
Our crafty group is a safe fun place for you to post
all your My Bestie Colorings, Creations, Photos,
Blog Posts, and More..... anything featuring our My
Besties Images, Stamps and Sherri Baldy Crafting
Products are welcome!
We have MANY Shops for you to enjoy featuring
Sherri Baldy My Bestie Craft Products!
Our My Bestie Shops:
www.MyBestiesShop.com
www.My-Besties.com
www.Scrapbookstampsociety.com

Our Etys Shop:
https://www.etsy.com/shop/SherriBaldy?ref=hdr_sh
op_menu

Join our Blog Challenges:

Our Sherri Baldy
Blog:http://sherribaldy.blogspot.com/

Sherri Baldy

Color With Sherri & The Besties!

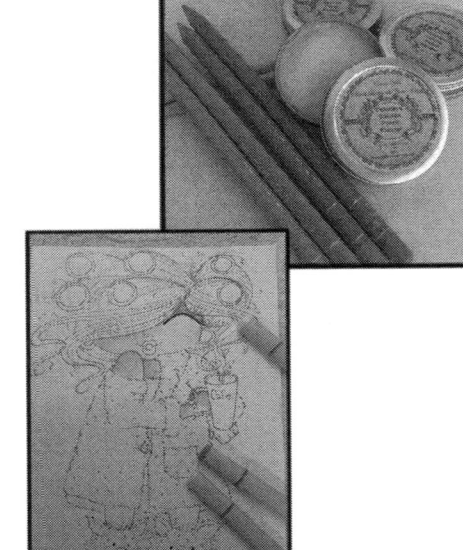

www.MyBestiesShop.com
Sherri Baldy My Besties Coloring Books in Riverside CA.
Copyright Sherri Baldy ~ My-Besties TM

I am so excited to introduce to you a new platform for My-Besties products. I wanted to create a place for my crafty friends, fans and collectors to meet up with me and interact in a whole new way. Members will be able to see and recieve new Bestie products before anyone else.

Come read about the different levels of membership on my patreon page here: patreon.com/SherriBaldy

Printable Coloring Books!

Digi Stamps & Coloring Pages!

Sneak Peeks!

In House Special Printed and signed Coloring Books!

Enamel Pins!

Made in the USA
Las Vegas, NV
23 June 2021